WORLD WAR II STORIES

WAR AT HOME

WORLD WAR II STORIES
WAR AT HOME

ANTHONY MASTERS

Illustrated by Joyce Macdonald

W

FRANKLIN WATTS

LONDON • SYDNEY

Text Editor Belinda Hollyer
Editor-in-Chief John C. Miles
Design Billin Design Solutions
Art Director Jonathan Hair

*The right of Anthony Masters to be identified as the
author of this work has been asserted.*

First published in 2004
by Franklin Watts
96 Leonard Street
London
EC2A 4XD

Franklin Watts Australia
45-51 Huntley Street
Alexandria
NSW 2015

ISBN 0 7496 4805 8

A CIP catalogue record for this book is available
from the British Library.

Printed in Great Britain

CONTENTS

PROLOGUE

In 1939, the German dictator, Adolf Hitler, invaded the Rhineland, Austria and Czechoslovakia without opposition. But when the Germans also marched into Poland, the Allies decided to try and stop them. On 3 September 1939, Britain and France declared war on Germany.

At first, the war went badly for the Allies. By June 1940 France had surrendered. Now most of Europe was occupied by the Germans. Britain stood alone, and under siege. German forces tried to make the British surrender by sinking the ships that brought vital supplies across the seas. Soon German aircraft bombed British cities as well. By May 1941, more than two million homes had been destroyed.

But the bombings and the shortages did not make the British give in. The bravery and spirit of co-operation amongst the British people – and their determination to keep their country running "no matter what" – all contributed to the eventual defeat of Germany in 1945.

For German Jews, the war at home began before World War II actually started. In 1935, the Nuremberg Laws were passed. These restrictions turned Jewish people into second-class citizens. By 1941 Jews were being deported from Germany, or sent to camps where they were worked to death. The "Final Solution" began in 1942. This involved the terrible death camps, which contributed to the deaths of around six million Jews.

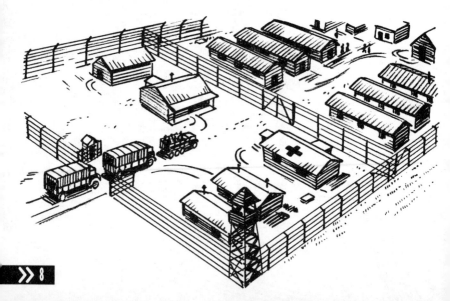

Throughout the war, intelligence – the gathering of information about the enemy – was of the highest importance. The more information about the enemy the British government could obtain, the more effectively they could act. Helping prisoners of war to escape – or even better, bringing soldiers home before they were captured – added essential information to the government's first-hand knowledge.

The intelligence teams did brilliant work, but Bletchley Park stood out above them all. Some of the cleverest people in the country worked at Bletchley Park. Without their genius for code-breaking, the British would not have won the war at sea. Thousands of lives would have been lost, and Britain would have been defeated.

WAR AT HOME

ESCAPE ROUTE

1. Do not march in a military style, but adopt a tired slouch.

2. Try to "collect" a bicycle.

3. Do not wear a wrist watch. Carry it in your pocket.

4. Sling your haversack over one shoulder. French peasants normally carry one in this way, but never as a pack on their backs.

5. Do not use a cane or walking stick. This is a British custom.

6. Get rid of army boots and adopt a pair of rope-soled shoes as worn by peasants, if procurable.

7. French peasants are usually clean-shaven, though a slight growth of beard is not uncommon.

8. A beret is a very effective disguise.

9. Village priests are likely to be helpful. Care should be exercised in approaching them and one should avoid being seen talking to them.

These instructions were contained in Major Norman Richard Crockatt's manual for training new recruits. He was 45 years old and an officer in the British Army. But he was also in charge of MI9, an important new branch of the British intelligence services.

Crockatt was well suited for the job. He had a brilliant record as a soldier during World War I. He was quick-witted, a good organiser and an excellent judge of character.

Major Crockatt's task was to create an underground network that would help British prisoners of war (POWs) escape from prison camps in German-occupied Europe, particularly France. This was not just a way to return valuable fighting men to the war effort. It was also a good way to pick up specialised knowledge of the enemy, which the POWs had gained. Crockatt also planned to help soldiers who had evaded capture, and were hiding in occupied territories, to return to Britain. That group of servicemen were ideally placed to collect and distribute information. They could even establish contacts in the prison camps, and help keep up morale among captured British POWs. In that way, POWs would be ready to escape if they found the opportunity.

At first, Major Crockatt worked with a very small team. But as the war continued, his team needed more and more recruits. At the MI9 training school, the would-be intelligence agents were instructed that no escaped POWs should try to make their own way to safety. Instead, they should wait

until a member of the "escape line" contacted them. This agent would help organise their escapes. Anyone hiding in enemy-occupied territory had to obey escape-line agents at all times.

The agents themselves were not allowed to speak to local people, or offer cigarettes or chocolates to anyone. Chocolate was unobtainable in Germany or the occupied countries at that time. Cigarettes were extremely scarce. Several escaped POWs had been identified by the nicotine stains on their forefingers.

The course leaders also explained some problems that had been caused by the inexperience or slow-thinking of some escapees. One British pilot was shot down near a French convent. Before he could be captured by the Germans, the pilot was rescued by a local escape-line contact, who whisked him away and hid him in the convent.

Next morning the pilot took a walk in the garden of the convent and saw a beautiful young nun. He approached her and began to speak to her, but his romantic advances were angrily brushed aside when the nun abruptly turned away and said in a deep masculine voice, "Don't be a fool. I've been here since early in the war!"

The escape-line agents were trained to give advice and practical help to the escapees. Clothing suitable to their new situation, and the right equipment, were both essential to their success.

The right clothes and equipment were also invaluable to prisoners who escaped from the POW camps. Red Cross parcels were an obvious way to send messages straight to the POWs, but Major Crockatt did not use the parcels as a message-carrying service because the Red Cross had an agreement with the Germans to remain neutral. However, parcels that contained equipment or clothes could be delivered through the Red Cross. In that way the Red Cross was only delivering innocent-looking parcels. If the Red Cross didn't know that secret devices were concealed inside ordinary objects, it didn't have to take responsibility for them.

Some of the objects posted inside Red Cross parcels were very cleverly concealed. In one case, a hacksaw blade was hidden in a toothbrush. In another, the handle of a cricket bat contained a screwdriver.

J. M. Langley was an early recruit to MI9 who helped the organisation enormously. He was a remarkable junior army officer, who had escaped from a hospital at Lille in

northern France in October 1940, despite
the fact that his left arm had been
amputated. He made his way to Marseilles
and then to London, where he joined
MI9. He became one of Crockatt's most
valuable intelligence officers, with special
responsibility for setting up escape lines.

MI9's headquarters was based in the
Broadway Buildings, opposite St James's
Park underground station in London.
A brass plate on the wall
outside claimed that
the building was the
Head Office of the
Minimax Fire Extinguisher
Company.

Another important
escape-line organiser
was a French-Canadian

sergeant-major, Lucien Dumais. He had been taken prisoner by the Germans in 1942, after the ill-fated landing by the Allies at Dieppe, in northern France, when many Canadian troops were killed. Lucien Dumais used a M19 escape line to return to Britain, where he quickly applied to join them.

His first meeting was conducted while he and his interviewer sat on a bench in bright sunshine in St James's Park. Dumais was asked whether he knew what he was letting himself in for. When he requested more information, his interviewer explained that once Dumais was employed as an escape-line contact in occupied France, MI9 could do nothing to help him. Indeed, as far as they were concerned, he would have ceased to exist.

The interviews continued over the next few weeks. MI9 also secretly arranged some incidents to test him. Dumais was approached in pubs by total strangers, who bought him drinks and tried to get him talking about what he did. On one occasion he was arrested on a false charge, and on another the military police accused Dumais of carrying forged identity papers.

Dumais became very angry, and insisted on laying a charge against the military police. But he was told to forget that idea, and had to learn to accept that he was continually being tested.

One morning, Lucien Dumais was told to report to the Free French headquarters and ask for a certain captain. (The Free French were based in London under Charles de Gaulle, and fought on with the Allies even though France had surrendered to Nazi Germany.) J. M. Langley was there to introduce Dumais to the officer, then he strolled away. The officer asked Dumais some loaded questions, and then insulted him, in French, by accusing him of wearing a medal to which he was not entitled. Dumais lost his temper.

"If you weren't in uniform," he said to

the Frenchman, "I'd fill you in!"

J. M. Langley stopped pretending to examine the pictures on the far wall, and walked back across the room.

"Cool down, Lucien," he said. "I just wanted to find out how good your French was. Now I know." Then he asked the

Frenchman for his opinion. The captain said Lucien Dumais's accent could be from central France, so a false life story was constructed accordingly.

Once accepted by MI9, Dumais began training as a parachutist. Later he picked up other skills, including learning how to throw off someone who was trailing him, and becoming a first-class pistol shot. Dumais was also taught to pick locks. The shooting practice was particularly challenging, and took place on a range beneath London's Baker Street Underground Station, in a room measuring 3 metres wide by 10 metres long. The space could hold only 10 men.

Shooting practice was a fast and furious business. One instructor would give the command to fire at a target, while another would try to distract the person who was shooting. The aim of the practice was to fire shots in pairs, very quickly.

Eventually, despite all distractions, Dumais and his fellow-trainees became very good at this.

At last, Dumais and a fellow agent were ready to parachute into occupied France. It was a great relief to be ready to go.

Both men were given various items to take with them – such as French money, compasses, tickets for the Paris underground and bus system, and road maps. Other vital tools were concealed inside their clothes, such as ropes coiled into the soles of their shoes. All MI9 missions were well-supplied. They were highly dangerous, and called for skills that could never be taught on the training courses. Successful escape-line agents were very brave, but above all else they had to be

resourceful, and keep cool under pressure
and in any emergency.

Many POWs, who might otherwise have spent years in prison camps, had good reason to be grateful to the escape-line agents. So did the Allies! Many POWs who were brought back to Britain in this way made very important contributions to Hitler's defeat.

WAR AT HOME
THE
BLITZ

For months beforehand, Londoners had feared what would happen. On 7 September 1940, their fears were realised. Waves of German bombers dropped their bombs on Woolwich Arsenal, on the gasworks at Beckton, on the docks, on West Ham's power station and three of the mainline railway stations – and on hundreds of private houses. The docks blazed on both banks of the River Thames. The sunlight paled beside the crimson glare that flickered over the East End.

That was just the beginning. During the next two months, London was bombed every night. By November 1940, many British ports, and many of the big provincial cities, also shared in the relentless nightly bombardment. But the British still refused to be crushed.

When the war began, the British government drew up plans to protect the general public. These plans were now put into operation, and everyone had a part to play. Windows had to be covered with thick curtains every night, and street lights were not allowed. That way, no light could be seen from the air which might help the German bombers to find their targets. This was called the black-out, and was

maintained throughout the war. Air-raid shelters – reinforced structures in which people could shelter from bombs – were built in public places, and people were encouraged to build their own shelters in their houses and gardens.

Ration books were issued so that food was shared out equally among the population, and gas masks were provided for everyone in case of a gas attack.

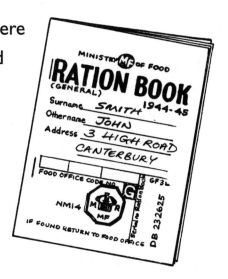

The Civil Defence network was set up to meet the population's personal and material needs. Some Civil Defence staff were responsible for dealing with the problems of the thousands of people affected by the nightly bombings. Others had to put out fires and make repairs to keep the essential services like gas, electricity and water supplies running. It was difficult and dangerous work.

Control centres for Civil Defence were set up in neighbourhoods all over Britain. These were used to get the right emergency services to each reported bomb incident as quickly as possible.

Some ordinary people found the crises created by the war were a welcome challenge. The sheer size of the problems and the difficulties brought out qualities and skills those people had never used before, and did not know they possessed. Working closely with others, in a common cause, banished loneliness. Finding solutions to important problems often raised people's self-esteem, and inspired them to carry out acts of outstanding bravery.

For others, however, it was a time of tragedy. City children were evacuated – sent into the countryside to save them from the bombing. Many of the children were very homesick, and some were sent to live with families who treated them badly.

Thousands of people died in the air-raids. Whole neighbourhoods were wiped out, and people lost their homes and all their possessions. But experiencing an air-raid could be exciting as well as frightening. This

survivor of the London air-raids has
fascinating memories to share:

"We were all really nervous that night
in the kitchen. Mum would say, 'Is that a
bomb?', and Dad would reply, 'No, it's just
gunfire. That's all it is. Just anti-aircraft guns.'
Mum could see he was getting irritated

and tried not to make things worse, muttering the question under her breath instead, which was more irritating than ever.

I felt all swollen up with irritation myself, bloated with it. But perhaps it was actually fear.

My brother Eddie must have felt the same way, because he whispered to me, 'Come on, Jenny. Let's get some air.'

Mum and Dad were arguing loudly by now. They didn't notice when we slipped outside. It was a perfect summer's night, so warm it was incredible. The night scene was made even more vivid by the red glow from the East End of London, where the docks were burning. I felt sorry for the East Enders. But still, I tried to fix the scene in my mind, because I knew this day would soon be history.

I wasn't so frightened out in the garden. The searchlights were beautiful. It was like watching the end of the world as they swept from one end of the sky to the other. We didn't see any planes, though we

could hear them. We sat on the grass, which was very long. Dad was usually a really keen gardener but, except for the vegetables, he'd let the garden go to rack and ruin. The bombs fell in the distance. I felt no fear, even though Eddie said he could smell burning from the docks. Another bomb. Nearer this time. Then, suddenly, there was the weirdest scratching sound just above the roofs of the houses – as if someone was scratching the sky with a broken fingernail. Then the most terrible crash – it seemed to be only a couple of gardens away. I felt the earth juddering under me as I sat there.

Suddenly Eddie exclaimed, 'Hey, it's not safe out here!' He dragged me up from the grass. I didn't seem to be doing anything – just sitting there, cowering.

I remember racing towards the house with Eddie pulling me and yelling. There was the oddest feeling in the air all around, as if the air itself was falling apart, quite silently. Suddenly I was on my face, just inside the kitchen. There seemed to be waves buffeting me, one after another, like bathing in a rough sea. I remember clutching at the floor, the carpet, to prevent myself being swept away. I could hear Mum screaming. The lights had gone out. It was all dust. I didn't even wonder if Eddie was all right... didn't even give him a thought. Couldn't give anything a thought. Seemed to be nothing in the universe but this dusty

carpet I was breathing into and having to
hang on to like grim death. I clutched the
floor as if it was a cliff-face. Mum seemed to
have been calling out for ages but I couldn't
answer her. I didn't think of answering or
doing anything about anything. It was almost
a tranquil feeling.

I could hear Dad yelling, 'Down, everybody, get down. Do what I tell you, get your heads down,' over and over again. There was no sense in it, because we'd had the bomb now and everybody was down, heads and all.

I managed to lift up my head from the carpet. I saw that Eddie had a torch and he was flashing it round the kitchen. Plaster and glass everywhere. Mountains of it. The whole ceiling had come down and it looked like a builder's yard. Dad was still shouting, giving orders. 'Don't move. Stay where you are! Someone tell the Hendersons next door. Don't move till I tell you!' and so on, and so on.

Somehow, we got to the front door, with Eddie in front. It was quite a job, as the ceilings had fallen down along the passage and everything was dark as pitch. I could hear Mum stumbling along behind with Dad scolding her, 'Watch out – can't you look where you're going?' each time she stumbled. Actually he was stumbling just as much and he was normally a good-natured sort of man who never raised his voice.

Looking back, I realise he must have been in shock. The front door was wedged tight and wouldn't budge. There were men outside and someone was saying in a high-pitched voice, 'Naomi, ask Naomi. Naomi will know. Has anyone seen Naomi?' I wondered vaguely who Naomi was and what she would know.

We went back into the parlour, as we couldn't get out through the front door. It wasn't so bad there. The ceiling had held and we crawled out through a broken window. It looked so bright outside I couldn't believe it. There was a sort of white haze, a halo over everything, though there was no moon. Two of the women standing outside cried when they saw us; how terrible we must have looked, smothered in white plaster and streaks of blood from the glass. 'Are you hurt... are

you hurt?' people kept asking us. It was only then that it occurred to me I might have been hurt... that I had been in real danger. Up to that minute I had taken everything for granted, in an odd, brainless way, as if it was all perfectly ordinary.

We spent the night at the Finches down the road. Mrs Finch insisted on putting about seven blankets on top of me, and a hot-water bottle as well. 'For the shock,' she said. When I pointed out I was feeling perfectly all right, she referred darkly to delayed shock, implying this dread phenomenon would hit me before the night was out. It didn't. I lay there feeling indescribably

happy and triumphant. 'I've been bombed,'
I kept saying to myself over and over again
– trying the phrase like a new dress, to see
how it fitted. 'I've been bombed – me!'
I was so glad to be alive. I felt as if I had
never been so glad in the whole of my life.
It seems a terrible thing to say when so
many must have been killed, but never in
my life have I experienced such pure and
flawless happiness."

Jenny was not alone in feeling special
as a result of her experience. Many people
who had led rather dull, routine lives got a
thrill from the dangers of war. When the
war was finally over, some people found
that they missed the excitement of the war
years. Then, they had responded brilliantly
to an extraordinary situation. Now, they

were just ordinary people again, living out their everyday lives in the safety – and the predictable routines – of peacetime.

WAR AT HOME

KRISTALL-NACHT

About 500,000 Jews lived in Germany before Adolf Hitler came to power in 1933. Hitler had raged against the Jews for many years, and now he could carry out many of his anti-Jewish policies. In 1935, the Nuremberg Laws took German citizenship away from Jewish people, and marriages between Jews and other German people were forbidden. But in 1938, life got even harder for the Jews.

On 9 November 1938, at about 9 p.m.,
Nazi leaders met to celebrate the fifteenth
anniversary of Adolf Hitler's rise to power.
But as they drank, the news came that a
Nazi official at the German Embassy in Paris
had been killed by a Jewish man. The man
was desperate at the news that his family
was to be deported. Hitler, furious, relied
on Joseph Goebbels, his propaganda chief,
to organise an effective retaliation that
would make German Jews the main target.

Goebbels seized the opportunity. A wave
of attacks on Jewish homes, synagogues,
shops and businesses began immediately,
which later became known as *Kristallnacht*
(the Night of Broken Glass).

Jewish communities have lived in most of
the big European cities since Roman times.
However, over the centuries, Jews were

often seen as "outsiders" in their own countries, and unfairly blamed for many problems. Sometimes entire Jewish communities were expelled from a city or even a country. European Jews never felt completely safe in their homes.

In spite of this history, Hitler's policy of persecution was a tremendous shock to German Jews. The Kristallnacht attacks took them by surprise, as the following stories show.

One evening, in Berlin, the Rosenfeld family were eating together and everything was very much as usual. But suddenly Ursula Rosenfeld found herself gazing at her father intensely, convinced she must imprint his image on her mind.

That night, nine-year-old Ursula dreamt that her father was being arrested. The next

morning she noticed there was a strange, rather eerie silence at breakfast. It was a relief to see that her father had not been arrested, but both her parents were very tense.

When Ursula arrived at school and went into the classroom, nobody said a word. All the pupils who normally chattered so loudly to one another were silent. The teacher, sounding nervous, took the register, and the first lesson started.

Just then, the whole class began to smell smoke. The school was opposite a small synagogue. The top floor was used for prayers, and there were two more rooms on the ground floor. One was the schoolroom, where Ursula had religious lessons twice a week. A Jewish family lived in the other room.

Now, as Ursula and the other children stared out at the synagogue, they saw flames flickering in its windows and smoke beginning to pour out from doorways.

The children and their teachers rushed out into the playground. Ursula saw in horror that the synagogue was alight! The streets were filled with people who were shouting and jeering and clapping at the blaze. But where were the family who lived in the synagogue? Had they escaped?

The street was in chaos. Ursula saw a doll lying face down near her feet. Further along, the pavement was strewn with furniture and clothes. The Jewish family's things had been thrown out of the window. It was terrible to see.

Then two men rushed out of the synagogue holding the Torah, the Jewish sacred book. The men were shouting mockingly, and dancing around with the book, tearing pages from it and stamping on them! Ursula could hardly believe what was happening.

"Stop! Stop right now!" she heard someone shout – and then she realised she had shouted it out. In that split-second, one of the men spun around and saw Ursula standing in the crowd of schoolchildren. "Let's get that dirty little Jew!" she heard.

At that, all the children standing in the playground turned and fled. On her way home, Ursula saw a Jewish man being dragged through the streets, but she still didn't understand what was going on.

When Ursula finally reached home she found their tidy, beautiful house in chaos.

Her mother was shaking, and her face looked grey. She told Ursula that her father had been arrested. Ursula's nightmare had come true.

Ursula never saw her father again. He was among the 20,000 Jews imprisoned by the Nazis after Kristallnacht. He was sent to Buchenwald – a forced-labour camp –

where men and boys worked twelve-hour shifts in local factories. They were allowed very little food, and almost no sleep or rest. They died from exhaustion, starvation and disease, at the rate of 6,000 deaths a month.

In contrast to Ursula's experience, Kurt Fuchel was with his parents when the Nazis evicted them from their home.

By coincidence, a few days before Kristallnacht, an interior decorator had taken a picture of the Fuchels' beautiful living-room and displayed it in his shop window. Unfortunately, a woman named Frau Januba had seen the picture, and had learnt that the apartment belonged to a Jewish family. She had gone to the Fuchels' apartment asking to buy it, but Frau Januba was told it was not for sale.

On the day that
was to erupt into
the violence
and looting of
Kristallnacht,
Frau Januba
returned to the

Fuchels' apartment. This time she was
accompanied by Nazi officials. She said the
apartment was now hers, and showed
Kurt's mother a Nazi legal document. She
told Kurt's mother that the whole family
would have to leave their home by 6 p.m.

Frau Fuchel cried and protested to the
Nazis that she had a sick child there, who
was sleeping. The Nazi officials relented
and agreed to let the Fuchel family stay
the night – although they would definitely
have to leave at 6 a.m. Next morning, a

triumphant Frau Januba bustled along to claim the Fuchels' apartment.

"You're stealing everything that my wife and I have worked for," Kurt's father protested angrily.

But Frau Januba only replied, "Stop talking like that or I'll have you sent to a concentration camp."

"You know this apartment isn't yours. You're a wicked woman!" Kurt yelled.

Frau Januba was simply furious. She told Kurt's parents to get him – and themselves – out of "her" apartment.

Despite the Fuchel family's protests, Frau Januba took over their home. There was, of course, no compensation for the Fuchel family. They were forced to move in with a Jewish neighbour who still had a house.

By 1939, more German Jews were being forced out of their homes. They were moved into the ghettos. At first, these were simply poor sections within German cities and towns. But the ghettos soon became strictly confined areas, in which Jews were imprisoned by the Nazis.

Some people understood what Kristallnacht meant more quickly than others. In Frankfurt, on the morning after Kristallnacht, Jack Hellman rode his bicycle to school as usual. But on his way he noticed smoke rising from two large synagogues, and saw the flames. Soon Jack realised that all the Jewish shops he passed had broken windows. Their stock had either been looted, or just lay scattered on the pavement. It was an appalling sight, and Jack felt very afraid.

When he arrived at school, the building was closed and he was told to go home. That wasn't easy for Jack because he had been sent to Frankfurt to be educated, and was living in a children's home. He cycled back to the home very frightened, hoping to catch up with his parents who had just been to visit him. But Jack's parents had already left for the railway station to return home. What should he do now?

Just then, his uncle telephoned with an urgent message for his parents.

"Tell your parents not to come home, Jack," said his uncle. "Their shop is in ruins, and there's nothing left of the apartment. All their furniture is lying in the street!"

Jack had no idea what time his parents' train would leave Frankfurt, but he desperately hoped they might still be at the station. He pedalled there furiously, but when he arrived there were only a few minutes to spare before the train left. Could he find them in time?

Jack pushed through the crowds and searched the station, but he couldn't see them anywhere. He almost gave up hope. Then suddenly, miraculously, he saw his parents standing on the platform – only about 20 metres away from him.

Jack told his parents about his uncle's telephone call and begged them not to go home. "Everything's in ruins," he said. "There's nothing there to return to!" But to Jack's dismay, his parents refused to stay. They simply couldn't believe his uncle's story, and they wanted to see for themselves.

At the children's home, the boys had a meeting and decided to take as many

knives and forks as they could get their hands on in order to defend themselves. They hid these in the bathroom. But they realised that knives and forks would be little use against the Nazis' guns.

The Nazis did not wait long. Soon afterwards they broke the windows of the children's home and arrested the house officers. They also arrested everyone who lived there who was between the ages of 16 and 65.

Jack was terrified. Even though he was only 12 so he wasn't arrested, he understood that there was no future for Jews in Nazi Germany. He knew that he had to escape – somehow.

Some Jews recognised how deep the Nazi's hatred for them had become. They understood that this political party intended to wipe them out, in all the lands it controlled. These Jews tried desperately to leave Germany. Others, however, simply couldn't believe that the country which had been their home for so long was now too dangerous for them.

Soon all German Jews were forced to accept that this was the case. Kristallnacht was only the beginning of the persecution.

By September 1939, nearly half of Germany's Jews had fled to other parts of Europe, or to the United States of America. But for the ones who were left, and for other Jews throughout Europe, much worse was to follow.

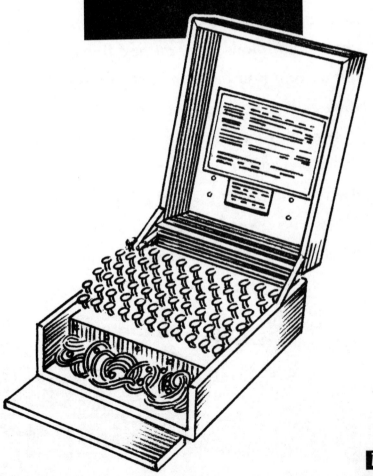

Cracking the Enigma code was the job of the Government Code and Cipher School, based at Bletchley Park, about 80 kilometres from London. The people at Bletchley were an unusual mixture of language specialists, mathematicians and chess champions. They all had first-class minds, and had been specially chosen for their skill in problem solving.

Bletchley Park was a beautiful old house, and it provided a luxurious environment for the code-breaking team. In the past, the family who owned the property had employed 40 gardeners to design and

maintain the gardens. There were many staff inside the house as well. It was still a very grand place, and even in wartime it was an attractive place to be. But none of the code-breakers had time to appreciate it. They urgently needed to concentrate on just one thing: breaking the Enigma code.

Enigma was used by Germany to send top secret messages to their most important naval officers. If Bletchley could intercept and understand the code, then Allied ships could avoid being attacked. The Allies would also be able to target German ships with deadly efficiency. Work on the Enigma code was Bletchley's most important war-time job.

One of the most famous code-breakers at Bletchley Park was Alan Turing. In private, he despaired of being able to crack the code, but he and his team kept hard at work. They knew that the Germans used a code-making machine – the Enigma machine – to put secret information and instructions into code. These messages could only be deciphered by using a similar machine, which turned the coded material back into ordinary language. The machines were, of course, tightly guarded, and only high-ranking German officers had access to them.

The Bletchley code-breakers did know that each of the German armed forces had been allocated a separate code. By early 1940, the coded messages sent to the air force and the army were regularly being broken by Alan Turing's team. But the code used to send messages to the navy – the naval Enigma code – was a far more difficult one to crack.

At the end of 1940, the Enigma code was still unbroken. The code-breakers desperately needed to get hold of one of the machines on which the code was produced. If they had a machine and could examine it minutely, perhaps they could work out how the impossibly complicated code had been created.

The need to plot the positions and monitor the movements of the German navy's U-boats had become urgent. After the war, Churchill summed up the situation by saying that the Battle of the Atlantic was the key to the whole war. Success in air and land battles, and even in sea battles in other places, was not as significant. The ultimate outcome of the war depended upon this battle – to keep the key Atlantic sea routes and ports open.

Without the ability to get food to the civilian population, and to the men and women who were fighting, Britain would have been starved into submission.

Churchill estimated that 31 million tons of supplies from abroad each year were essential. That would feed the British population, run the factories, and feed and equip the fighting forces. But in the first few months of 1941, it was estimated that only

28 million tons of foreign supplies would reach Britain safely. Worse still, Germany's U-boats were sinking Allied ships more quickly than Britain and the United States of America could build new ones to replace them. The situation was very grim.

Then, in early 1941, there was an unexpected breakthrough.

Under cover of a raid on Norway, British commandos (elite troops) attacked and damaged a German trawler called the *Krebs*. A boarding party searched the burning ship, and when they broke open a locked drawer the commandos found two discs for a code machine. They also found a document which

turned out to be the Enigma code's settings for the month of February.

On 9 May 1941, a second discovery was made. A German U-boat attacked a convoy of merchant ships, which was being escorted across the Atlantic by eight British warships. The escort commander, Joe Baker-Creswell, was able to outmanoeuvre and damage the U-boat. When the German crew then abandoned ship, the commander seized his opportunity.

All British naval commanders had been instructed to rescue cipher machines and code-books from captured enemy ships. The commander put a 22-year-old sub-lieutenant, David Balme, in charge of a boarding party. He told him to look for, and bring back, any code books he could find on the German U-boat.

Sub-lieutenant Balme found that the U-boat was in a terrible state, and might sink at any moment. But he quickly saw that it was full of code material that would be a treasure trove for the British. He realised there was no time to lose. Papers, books and charts lay everywhere, so Balme turned his boarding party into a human chain. Down below in the U-boat, important

documents were quickly passed from
person to person, up to those on deck.
Then Balme's radio operator called out to
him. "Here's something interesting I want to
show you!" Underneath the table in the
radio room was a machine that looked
rather like a
typewriter. At last
they had found an
Enigma machine.

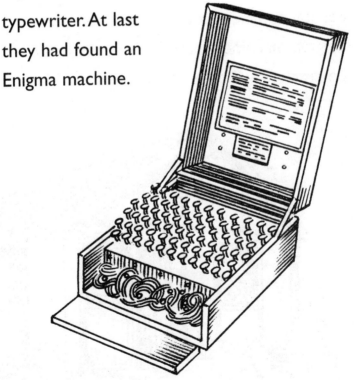

Back at Bletchley, the code-breakers made good use of the U-boat finds. The code-breakers were grouped in huts in the grounds of the mansion, and each group worked on a different problem. In Hut Eight, Alan Turing had already invented a code-breaking machine. But the Germans constantly changed the settings on the Enigma machines. Each day's codes had to be cracked swiftly – and Turing's machine,

ingenious though it was, worked very slowly. But Gordon Welchman, a brilliant Cambridge mathematician in Hut Six, managed to improve Turing's design to make it twice as quick. Then Turing, in turn, did even better. He improved on Welchman's improvement of his original design, and doubled the speed of the process yet again.

Some of the cleverest people in Britain had been recruited to work at Bletchley Park, and many of them were very young.

Alan Turing had become a Fellow of King's College, Cambridge, when he was only 22. His colleague Richard Pendered was only in his first year at Cambridge when he joined Bletchley Park.

He went to the factory where Turing's new machine was being built, and ran a code-breaking test. The process was painfully slow, but eventually the machine produced a setting. Pendered took it away to a private room to analyse it on his own. He spent days testing and re-testing, and finally managed to key in a sequence of numbers that made the machine produce some words in German. Pendered knew, at last, that he had found the basics of a way to break the code.

Harry Hinsley, also 22, made an important contribution to the work at Bletchley Park. He worked in the naval intelligence section in Hut Four. His job was to check the flow of German communications and note any variation in their patterns. A variation might show that some special activity was about to take place.

By June 1940, Hinsley was warning the Admiralty's Operational Intelligence Centre (OIC) that German warships were now in Norwegian waters. They were a serious danger to British ships in the North Sea, because the German code-breakers could read the Royal Navy's codes and discover where British ships were.

The OIC ignored Hinsley's warnings. As a result, two German battle cruisers – the *Gneisenau* and the *Scharnhorst* – trapped the British aircraft carrier HMS *Glorious*. The *Glorious* was sunk, along with her two accompanying destroyers, and many sailors were killed.

The personnel at OIC finally realised they should have listened to Harry Hinsley.

From then on Hinsley's work was taken very seriously. In the spring of 1941, one of his flashes of genius produced a further breakthrough in the battle to solve the Enigma code.

Harry Hinsley knew that the Germans sent out weather reports to their fleet in code. He also knew that the weather ships were isolated and unprotected – a serious lapse in German security. So Hinsley suggested that a German weather ship should be captured. His idea was put into action, and the weather code together with the Enigma settings for the month of June were successfully captured from the weather ship, *Munchen*. This information was invaluable to Bletchley.

The main problem remaining was that the Enigma settings were changed daily, and so from Bletchley's point of view the information they contained was always out of date. But on 13 December 1942, the Bletchley teams discovered that the key to the position of German U-boats involved weather forecasts with secret information buried in them. Later that day came the next breakthrough, as solutions to the Enigma code (code-named "Shark" by the Bletchley team) began to emerge. The triumphant members of the Bletchley Park team called the Submarine Tracking Station to report their breakthrough. In just one hour, the positions of 15 U-boats were revealed. More U-boat positions were located throughout the following night.

At last, British convoys could be re-routed. In January and February 1943, the number of British ships sunk was halved.

By February 1943, Admiral Doenitz, who commanded Germany's U-boats, had become suspicious that his codes were being cracked. For two-and-a-half weeks in January, German U-boats patrolling the North Atlantic sea routes to Britain hadn't discovered any British convoys. The British convoys must be changing direction and avoiding the U-boats.

Doenitz couldn't believe that the Allies had cracked the Enigma code. He wrote in his diary that enemy information about the positions of German U-boats seemed to have been obtained by the use of airborne radar. He was convinced that the enemy had "an extraordinary location device, usable from aeroplanes, whose effect cannot be observed by our boats."

Doenitz had been misinformed. As time went by, and more British convoys escaped, he became more suspicious. He even fired the adviser who had assured him that the Enigma codes were still secure. But the new adviser also believed that Enigma could not be cracked.

Admiral Doenitz and his advisers had underestimated the dedication and persistence of the British code-breakers. Bletchley Park brought together a wide range of people, whose brilliant minds thrived on problem-solving. Without their genius the vital Enigma code would never have been broken, and Britain would probably have been forced to surrender.

GLOSSARY

Allies
Countries such as Britain, France and the USA that fought together against Germany, Japan, Italy and some other countries during World War II.

Aircraft carrier
A large ship with an immense top deck, on which aircraft can take off and land.

Concentration camps
Prison camps where European Jews (and other groups, such as gypsies) were held by the Nazis in terrible conditions. Most inmates were murdered, or died of disease and starvation.

Dictator
A leader who imposes his will on a country using military force and intimidation instead of elections.

Free French
The French fighters who fought with the Allies after France had surrendered to the Germans.

Kristallnacht ("Night of the Broken Glass")
The night of 9-10 November 1938, when Nazis attacked Jewish synagogues, businesses and homes.

Nazi

A member of Adolf Hitler's National Socialist Party and supporter of its policies.

POW

Short for "prisoner of war". A member of a country's armed forces captured by the enemy in battle or in enemy territory.

Red Cross

An international humanitarian organisation set up to provide emergency help around the world, to anyone who needs it.

Swastika

An ancient symbol of a twisted cross that was used as the emblem of the Nazi Party.

Synagogue

A Jewish place of worship.

U-boat

U-boat is a translation from the German of U-boot. It is short for Unterseeboot or an undersea boat.

WAR AT SEA

The enemy was all around. The Luftwaffe (the German air force), the U-boats and the warships of the German navy all lay in wait. And there were always the icebergs, and the freezing fog, of the Barents Sea.

WAR ON LAND

The first wave of troops was mostly killed, cut down as they came ashore. Then the second wave of troops had to advance over the bodies of the dead. Survival was their main instinct.

WAR AT HOME

The boys had a meeting and decided to take as many knives and forks as they could get their hands on in order to defend themselves. But they realised that knives and forks would be little use against the Nazis' guns.

WAR IN THE AIR

Dundas's Spitfire began to spiral downwards, spinning wildly while he pulled and wrenched and hammered at the hood to open it. But Dundas still couldn't get the canopy open wide enough to escape through the gap.